THIS IS ME! ACROSTICS

Poetic Gems

Edited By Debbie Killingworth

First published in Great Britain in 2022 by:

Young Writers
Remus House
Coltsfoot Drive
Peterborough
PE2 9BF
Telephone: 01733 890066
Website: www.youngwriters.co.uk

All Rights Reserved
Book Design by Ashley Janson
© Copyright Contributors 2022
Softback ISBN 978-1-80015-137-6

Printed and bound in the UK by BookPrintingUK
Website: www.bookprintinguk.com
YB0517L

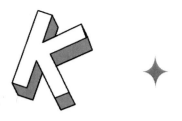

Foreword

Welcome Reader,

For Young Writers' latest competition *This Is Me Acrostics*, we asked primary school pupils to look inside themselves, to think about what makes them unique, and then write an acrostic poem about it! They rose to the challenge magnificently and the result is this fantastic collection of poems, celebrating them and the things that are important to them.

Here at Young Writers our aim is to encourage creativity in children and to inspire a love of the written word, so it's great to get such an amazing response, with some absolutely fantastic poems. It's important for children to focus on and celebrate themselves and this competition allowed them to write freely and honestly, celebrating what makes them great, expressing their hopes and fears, or simply writing about their favourite things. *This Is Me Acrostics* gave them the power of words.

I'd like to congratulate all the young poets in this anthology, I hope this inspires them to continue with their creative writing.

Contents

Jordanhill School, Glasgow

Max Christie (7)	62
Catrin Ogle (8)	63
Alexis Nairn (7)	64
Ayva Kyle (7)	65
Rory Farquhar (8)	66
Florence Duthie (8)	67
Isabella Lewin (7)	68
Maisie Black (8)	69
Ryan D'Sa (7)	70
Harrison Crichton (8)	71
Zoe Fleming (7)	72
James MacLeod (7)	73
Annabel McCrosson (7)	74
Seb McKenna (7)	75
Imogen Watson (8)	76
James McCrea (8)	77
Murray Munro (8)	78
Raya McLaughlin (7)	79
Aidan McLaughlin (7)	80
Zara Patel (7)	81
Arran Bailey (7)	82
Brody Doran (7)	83
Freya Mackay (7)	84
Eva Dougan (8)	85
Sam McDonald (7)	86
Seamus Farrell (7)	87
Lawrie Nairn (7)	88
Sara Aslam (7)	89
Thomas Burke (8)	90
Alexander Matheson (7)	91
Arwen Gilmour (7)	92
Erik Tilston (7)	93
Chloe Turnbull (7)	94

St John's CE School, Stanmore

Dulcine-Vittoria Dubceac (6)	95
Reheem Khan (7)	96
Deumini Kolonne Appuhamillage (5)	97
Emma Stone (7)	98
Rio Reyes-Francis (6)	99

Agastya Panwar (6)	100
Sophia Murphy (6)	101
Sebastian Onate (6)	102
David Alexandru (6)	103
Alexander Boghian (7)	104
Iustina Chelaru (6)	105
Ava-Grace Lucien (7)	106
Aaliyah Perkins (6)	107
Ishaan Wara (6)	108
Aileen Grigore (7)	109
Eli Nistor (7)	110
Bhavik Benoi (5)	111
Zaynab Moledina (7)	112
Chisom Eziefula (7)	113
Anna-Maria Matyas (6)	114
Lydia Tapp (7)	115
Reign Maleek Huie (6)	116
Nicolas Gavril (6)	117
Alexandru Buburuza (7)	118
Noble Owusu Nyamekye (6)	119
James Nicoll (6)	120
Aadya Mishra (6)	121
Damian Pascal (6)	122
Eva Brindusoiu (6)	123
James Sav (6)	124
Shaheem Ramzan (7)	125
Kulthum Moledina (7)	126
Ameliya Powell Clarke	127
Rayan McAlister (6)	128
Damaris Vladean (7)	129
Keziah O (6)	130
George Raine (6)	131

Wincham Community Primary School, Wincham

Urwa Azmat (7)	132
Rory Harris (7)	133
Hugo Moorhouse (7)	134
Sebastian Fitzsimmons (6)	135
Lucy Stainsby (7)	136
Oliver Earl (7)	137
Callum Scott (6)	138
Joshua Southern (6)	139

The
Acrostics

Auriella

A uriella is my name.
U nbelievable.
R ed is my favourite colour.
I ce cream.
E ggs are yummy.
L ovely girl.
L ove ice cream.
A lways kind.

Auriella Prothero (5)
Deighton Primary School, Tredegar

Marli-Paige

M arvellous
A lways happy
R uby
L ove
I ce cream
-
P arty
A pples
I ncredible
G irl
E xcited.

Marli-Paige Pearce (4)
Deighton Primary School, Tredegar

Fiola-Mae

F abulous

I ce cream

O ranges

L ike my friends

A pples

-

M am

A mbitious

E ggs.

Fiola-Mae Watkins (4)

Deighton Primary School, Tredegar

Jessica

J essica is my name.

E ggs are my favourite food.

S weeties are

S uper.

I like Mum.

C aring.

A pples.

Jessica Ladyga (5)

Deighton Primary School, Tredegar

Paisleigh

P aisleigh

A pple

I ce cream

S weets

L ove

E xcited

I ce

G ood girl

H appy.

Paisleigh Caddick (4)

Deighton Primary School, Tredegar

Jackson

J ackson is my name.
A mbitious.
C ats are lovely.
K ing.
S nakes.
O n the pitch.
N ice and kind.

Jackson Holly (5)
Deighton Primary School, Tredegar

Jaxson

J axson is my name.

A pples are yummy.

e **X** ercise.

S nakes

O range.

N ice and kind.

Jaxson Beattie (5)

Deighton Primary School, Tredegar

Freddie

F reddie

R unning

E ats ice cream

D ogs

D reamer

I ce cream

E xcited.

Freddie Jones (4)

Deighton Primary School, Tredegar

Lincoln

L incoln

I ce cream

N ice

C ool

O ne of me

L ove

N oisy.

Lincoln Foote (5)

Deighton Primary School, Tredegar

Reggie

R eggie is my name

E ggs

G reat

G reen eyes

I ce cream

E xcellent.

Reggie Pritchard (4)
Deighton Primary School, Tredegar

Reuben

R euben

E xercise

U nder the table

B rother

E ggs

N ice smile.

Reuben Willis (5)

Deighton Primary School, Tredegar

Freddi

F reddi
R espectful
E ating
D ogs
D ancing
I ce cream.

Freddi Evans (4)
Deighton Primary School, Tredegar

Rosie

R osie is my name

O ranges

S weet girl

I ce cream

E nergetic.

Rosie Taylor (5)

Deighton Primary School, Tredegar

Angelo

A rtistic

N ice

G orgeous

E ggs

L ovely

O ranges.

Angelo Cowdell (5)

Deighton Primary School, Tredegar

Olivia

O livia

L ovely

I ce

V ibrant

I ce cream

A pples.

Olivia Hayman (5)

Deighton Primary School, Tredegar

Kayla

K ayla
A lways smiling
Y ellow
L ovely
A pples.

Kayla Watson (5)

Deighton Primary School, Tredegar

Tayla

T ayla
A lways happy
Y ellow
L ovely
A wesome.

Tayla Scott (5)
Deighton Primary School, Tredegar

Codie

C odie

O ranges

D ad

I ce cream

E nergetic.

Codie Barnett (5)

Deighton Primary School, Tredegar

Jack

J ack is my name.
A pples are healthy.
C lever.
K ing.

Jack Brewer (5)

Deighton Primary School, Tredegar

Poppy

P retty

O ranges

P ink

P recious

Y ellow.

Poppy Pope (4)

Deighton Primary School, Tredegar

Jacob

J acob
A wesome
C ake
O ranges
B atman.

Jacob Williams (5)
Deighton Primary School, Tredegar

Afia

A fia is my name

F ast

I ce cream

A pple.

Afia Turner (5)

Deighton Primary School, Tredegar

Mya

M ya is my name
Y ummy doughnuts
A lways smiling.

Mya Williams (5)

Deighton Primary School, Tredegar

Isla

I sla

S uper

L ovely

A lways happy.

Isla Hughes (4)

Deighton Primary School, Tredegar

JayT

J ayT
A wesome
Y ellow
T oast.

JayT Howells (5)
Deighton Primary School, Tredegar

Jack

J ack
A wesome
C ake
K ind.

Jack Davies (5)
Deighton Primary School, Tredegar

This Is Me

P erfect stem with hairy fur

O pposite of rubbish, more like stunning!

P early-white and black glittery centre

P eople like its fluorescent red petals

Y ellow of the sun shining down upon.

F lowers like poppies have pollen and bees take a little of it for honey. "I am hungry," says the bee!

L ight that makes shadows of it.

O h it is a lovely red.

W ow what a great picture you can get.

E lectric lightbulbs are not lighter than their colour.

R ainbow - red is the first colour of that.

Poppy Anderson-Humphrey (6)

Didcot Primary Academy, Great Western Park

Sia Gokhale - Me

S ummer is my favourite season.
I love to go to the pool.
A mazing time to play with my friends.

G ardens growing with beautiful flowers.
O utdoors is what I like.
K oalas are my favourite animal.
H ome with my family.
A wesome family around the world.
L oving sister.
E nergetic little girl.

M agic tricks I learn all the time.
E verything is me.

Sia Gokhale (6)
Didcot Primary Academy, Great Western Park

Brother

B ouncing up and down in his jumper, that's my baby brother.

R alph is his name, that's my little brother.

O n his wheelie bug panda, this is one of his favourite toys.

T alking about my day my brother listens and smiles.

H enry is his elder brother.

E ating a dinner of scrambled eggs is his favourite.

R esting peacefully in his cot, it's time to say goodnight.

Henry Pether (7)
Didcot Primary Academy, Great Western Park

Rainbow

R aindrops fall down through the day.
A lthough the weather changes day by day.
I n the sun you can go to a nice place.
N othing compared to the weather today
B ut the sun is out for you to play.
O r if you are not in the mood you can always read your favourite book!
W hatever makes you happy, it is your choice.

Zena N'Jie (7)

Didcot Primary Academy, Great Western Park

Butterfly

B eautiful

U nbelievable at flying

T ransformation from a caterpillar to a butterfly

T ricks can be played on you with their wings

E legant and gracious

R ising up and up they flutter

F lying can be done easily for them

L ovely creatures

Y ears pass quickly but more and more come out.

Eva Sagoo (6)

Didcot Primary Academy, Great Western Park

Mia Allens

M y life is a gift.

I am a star.

A lways shining like a diamond.

A s a student I am kind.

L ove to help anyone in need.

L oves gardening and removing weeds.

E gg and mayo sandwiches are my fave.

N ot forgetting juice that I crave.

S o thankful to be the girl that I am.

Mia Allens (6)

Didcot Primary Academy, Great Western Park

Taha

T all and fair in colour.
A ctive and do things really fast.
H elp others and make them happy.
A pples are my favourite fruit.

F ruity and very juicy.
R ich in vitamins.
U seful for everyone.
I like fruits very much.
T asty, everyone loves to eat fruit.

Taha Jawad (7)
Didcot Primary Academy, Great Western Park

This Is Me

S lime is fun.
I ce cream is yummy.
E verything is beautiful.
N ow I'm six.
N ow I do dancing.
A pples are the best.

M um is amazing.
I 'm beautiful.
L ottie is amazing.
L ambs are brilliant.
S lides are fun.

Sienna Mills (6)
Didcot Primary Academy, Great Western Park

All About Me

F antastic, feisty rugby player.

E xcellent, energetic swimmer.

L oving all my lessons.

I ce cream on a hot day is a treat for me.

C reative, colourful creator.

I ndependent mathematician.

T errific, talkative friend.

Y ellow is my school house colour.

Felicity Hall (7)

Didcot Primary Academy, Great Western Park

Flowers

F lowers grow tall in spring.

L eaves change colour in autumn.

O utside there are lots of different coloured flowers.

W ater helps flowers grow.

E very flower lives happily under the bright sun.

R oses are lovely and beautiful.

S eeds make flowers.

Ava Edwards (5)

Didcot Primary Academy, Great Western Park

Rebecca

R unning keeps me strong and big.

E ating healthy food is good.

B eats and music makes me proud and happy.

E arly bedtime is bad for you.

C uts are nasty.

C reative art is what I do.

A ll those words are what keeps me healthy.

Rebecca Woodward (6)

Didcot Primary Academy, Great Western Park

A Day On The Beach

W indy days on the beach,
E njoying a chocolate ice cream,
Y ummy yum yum!
M eeting my friends on the sand,
O cean waves,
U nder the sun together,
T ippy-toeing in the water.
H ome after a happy day.

Felicity Quinn (6)
Didcot Primary Academy, Great Western Park

My Favourite Things

C ats are cute.

A ctive at night.

T is for tail.

A pples are different colours.

P eel off the skin and eat it.

P ut in the basket.

L eave them in the fridge.

E veryone likes them.

Safa Jawad (6)

Didcot Primary Academy, Great Western Park

Ollie's Football Poem

F eet are what we use to move the ball.

O n the pitch I feel happy.

O ffside rule.

T eammates.

B all boy.

A ttacker.

L ike playing for Didcot Town.

L eft-wing is where I play.

Oliver Robinson (7)

Didcot Primary Academy, Great Western Park

About Me

J ust loves gymnastics.

A nimal lover.

S uper smart superstar.

M y headstands are getting better.

I lost eight teeth.

N ever forget my BFF.

E veryone is my friend.

Jasmine Gill (6)

Didcot Primary Academy, Great Western Park

Yummy Ice Cream

I cy cold.

C urly, licking tongue.

E pic taste.

C ooling treat.

R efreshing snack.

E njoy it in a cone.

A ny sauce?

M y favourite summer treat!

Rufus Haskell-Watkins (7)

Didcot Primary Academy, Great Western Park

Phoebe

P andas are my favourite.

H ome is my safe place.

O ctopuses are my favourite sea creature.

E els can be electric.

B irds fly in the sky.

E lephants are big.

Phoebe Charlesworth (6)

Didcot Primary Academy, Great Western Park

Nature

N ests in a tree.

A pples growing on trees.

T he leaves are falling.

U p in the sky birds fly high.

R akes clean the leaves.

E veryone enjoys the garden.

Seren Woollard (6)

Didcot Primary Academy, Great Western Park

Spring

S plendid sunshine in spring.

P retty flowers blossoming.

R ainbows fill the sky.

I nsects and butterflies.

N ature sings a song.

G rass grows very long.

Mitch Coxon (8)

Didcot Primary Academy, Great Western Park

I Am Inesh

I am Inesh and I like Mario

N ew to Luigi's mansion 3

E ven Kirby games.

S o I also like Sonic the Hedgehog.

H edgehogs are very spiky but this one's blue.

Inesh Ratnala (7)

Didcot Primary Academy, Great Western Park

Outside

J umping around in the garden.

O utside.

S eagulls fly in the sky.

E verywhere flowers have powers.

P retty colours.

H ot sun in the sky makes it fun.

Joseph Hill (6)

Didcot Primary Academy, Great Western Park

Ellie's Life

E llie is encouraging to others.

L oyal to my friends.

L oving to friends and family.

I nspiring people to be kind and brilliant.

E njoying life and having fun.

Ellie Godfrey (5)

Didcot Primary Academy, Great Western Park

Alice

A weird girl that tries to be helpful.
L oves being kind.
I nterested in almost everything.
C ake is my favourite food.
E lephants are my favourite animals.

Alice Rush (7)
Didcot Primary Academy, Great Western Park

This Is Me

H arriet is kind

A n amazing child

R unning is fun

R ainbows are so fun

I am seven years old

E xciting world

T ime to say goodbye.

Harriet Franklin (7)

Didcot Primary Academy, Great Western Park

Music

M elody is relaxing music.

U kulele makes good music.

S inging and dancing.

I magine that the music is everywhere.

C olourful music is colourful.

Leon Pochopien (7)

Didcot Primary Academy, Great Western Park

The Reading Train

T ravelling through the trees.
R hys was reading his book.
A man checks my ticket.
I was staring out the window.
N ow we arrive at Reading.

Elliot McKelvey (6)

Didcot Primary Academy, Great Western Park

Elvin Poem

E ggs are my favourite food

L amb is my favourite sandwich

V an is my favourite car

I s it your favourite too?

N ature is my favourite too.

Elvin Zarei (5)

Didcot Primary Academy, Great Western Park

Kyra

K inder chocolate I love to eat.

Y oghurt makes me want to freeze.

R ipe apples are yummy to eat.

A hope would be to have something lovely to eat.

Kyra Bhanushali (6)

Didcot Primary Academy, Great Western Park

All About Incredible Me

C lara is kind and brilliant.

L ooking after my pet dog.

A n amazing girl.

R ainbows is my favourite club.

A t school I like to learn.

Clara Franklin (7)

Didcot Primary Academy, Great Western Park

Eloise

E njoys gymnastics.

L oves koalas.

O ranges are yummy.

I s good at reading.

S inging is good.

E ggs are scrumptious.

Eloise Chown (6)

Didcot Primary Academy, Great Western Park

Rabbit

R uns with speed.

A wesome looking.

B ouncing along.

B right colourful eyes.

I nteresting as a pet.

T oes are cute.

Albert Tawiah (6)
Didcot Primary Academy, Great Western Park

Amazing Fairy

F riendly fairy

A lways helping

I n Fairyland and

R iding flying horses

Y ou might see one if you believe.

Naomi Day (5)
Didcot Primary Academy, Great Western Park

Bees

B ees buzz around.

E verywhere the bees fly.

E ach bee collects honey from flowers.

S tores honey to form honeycomb.

Adithya Satram (5)

Didcot Primary Academy, Great Western Park

Roman

R eally cool boy
O nly five
M akes lots of noise
A nd loves to jive
N ever rude and always kind.

Roman Varney (5)
Didcot Primary Academy, Great Western Park

Cleo

C aterpillars are wriggly.

L eaves are their best food.

E ach one makes a cocoon.

O ut pops a butterfly.

Cleo Crossman (6)

Didcot Primary Academy, Great Western Park

Max Joseph

M y most important favourite game is Roblox.

A mazing black pudding with tattie scones for breakfast.

e **X** hausting running.

J uice with no bits is ultra good.

O utside skateboarding on my cousin's skateboard.

S unny Spain is my out-of-this-world holiday.

E xcellent swimming.

P laces I like and where I want to go... London, France and I've been to Spain.

H aving fun.

Max Christie (7)
Jordanhill School, Glasgow

Catrin

C limbing is fun and wonderful, I can go so high, it is amazing on top of the wall.

A rt is another one of my hobbies, I love doing art with friends.

T errific Minecraft is really fun and amazing, you can do lots of stuff.

R emember that I am nice and funny.

I love giraffes, they are incredible with their long necks.

N ow yellow is my favourite colour, I love it because it is the colour of the sun.

Catrin Ogle (8)

Jordanhill School, Glasgow

Alexis

A lexis is my name, I have brown eyes and dark brown hair.

L awrie is my twin brother, Isla is my big sister and Christie is my baby brother.

E mma is my friend forever, we play every day together.

X mas is my favourite time of the year with Santa and my elf.

I like purple, art, cats, music and dancing, I also like cycling.

S o that is me, it is nice meeting you, it was nice of you to come by!

Alexis Nairn (7)
Jordanhill School, Glasgow

Gymnastics

G ymnastics is my favourite hobby.

Y ou will never stop it.

M y favourite move in gymnastics is a handstand.

N ice people are at gymnastics.

A mazing tricks you can do in gymnastics.

S winging on the bars.

T he coaches are really nice.

I like gymnastics so much.

C razy trampolines are bouncy.

S itting on the tracks and listening.

Ayva Kyle (7)
Jordanhill School, Glasgow

Football

F ootball is my favourite sport, I just love it.

O ur football team that I play for is called BSC.

O n Monday, Wednesday and Saturday I play with my team.

T imes I play... 6-7pm on weekdays and 9-10am on Saturday.

B efore I go I have breakfast and get changed

A nd our kit is blue.

L ucas is someone in my team.

L isten, our team is good.

Rory Farquhar (8)
Jordanhill School, Glasgow

Florence

F lorence is my fantastic name.

L ove cheesy homemade pizza.

O ne of my fantastic, kind friends is Martha.

R upert is my cat's name.

E lephants are big, powerful and strong and that is why they are my favourite animal.

N ice people are my favourite people.

C heeky yes, that is me, I am very cheeky.

E veryone is unique just like me.

Florence Duthie (8)
Jordanhill School, Glasgow

Happy

H i, I am Isabella and I adore my family and my pet cat, Harvey, who is black and white.

A happy little girl named Jessica is my sister and I adore her.

P ersonally, I think art and swimming are my favourite hobbies.

P arty food that my dad makes is scrumptious.

Y es, how did you guess that school is my favourite place and pink is my favourite colour?

Isabella Lewin (7)
Jordanhill School, Glasgow

Maisie

M y amazing family is awesome.

A ctive things are my thing.

I love my mummy, daddy and my sister.

S is and me sometimes get along and sometimes we hate each other.

I nteractive me, I am unique because of my hair, it's all fluffy and scruffy.

E xciting, intelligent me, I already know my divisions and I like street dancing.

Maisie Black (8)

Jordanhill School, Glasgow

Swimming

S wimming is one of my favourite sports.

W inding my hands forwards and backwards.

I really like putting my hands in circles.

M y mum likes the front crawl.

M y second favourite is back crawl.

I love when I can put my head in the water.

N ight is when I dream of swimming. I've

G ot great friends.

Ryan D'Sa (7)

Jordanhill School, Glasgow

Motorbike

M ost of my bikes are petrol
O h I love the revving sound
T he road motorbike goes the fastest
O h they are different colours
R eally fast, my bike goes very fast
B ikes are super fun
I have three bikes to ride
K ick start the engine, that's what you do
E veryone can enjoy them.

Harrison Crichton (8)

Jordanhill School, Glasgow

Climbing

C limbing is fun.
L ingering in trees looking at the view.
I 'm so happy climbing.
M y body is tired from climbing all day.
B ouncing on trees, trying to get higher.
I 'm great at climbing to the top.
N o stopping until I get to the top.
G reat, I'm going to get a climbing frame.

Zoe Fleming (7)
Jordanhill School, Glasgow

James

J ames is my name, I like jam and ketchup.

A t the park my favourite thing is the monkey bars.

M y thing when I grow up is to be a footballer.

E very day of school my favourite work is numeracy, our topic and art.

S uper days on the weekend, free time, no school and you can spend time with family.

James MacLeod (7)
Jordanhill School, Glasgow

Annabel

A nnabel is my name, I love hockey.

N ew things make me scared and I am funny.

N ext year I will be in Primary 4.

A puppy is my favourite animal.

B russels sprouts are a vegetable I don't like.

E mma is my friend, she is very clever.

L oving my mum and dad all the time.

Annabel McCrosson (7)
Jordanhill School, Glasgow

Quokka

Q uokkas have curly, fluffy and cute skin.

U nlikely but they have pouches like kangaroos.

O nly they live in the bottom of Australia.

K angaroos and quokkas are my two favourite animals.

K ind of they smile even when they are sad.

A mazing, happy marsupials live in Australia.

Seb McKenna (7)
Jordanhill School, Glasgow

Imogen

I like swimming, I'm funny, happy and active.

M y hair is blonde, I think it suits me.

O n my birthday it's springtime.

G ymnastics is my favourite hobby, I'm really good at cartwheels.

E very day I am excited to go to school.

N ever have I ever made someone sad.

Imogen Watson (8)

Jordanhill School, Glasgow

Balls

F ootball is a very fun sport.

O utside I play football.

O n Thursdays I play.

T oday I play football.

B ut I play in defence which is fun.

A very fun sport that I like.

L ovely sport that gets you fit.

L ike this sport because it gets me active.

James McCrea (8)

Jordanhill School, Glasgow

YoungWriters

Murray

M y name is Murray and this is what I do...

U nique people - everyone is unique like me and I play tennis.

R eally the best thing about my life is my family.

R iding is fun but I need some TV time.

A rt is fun because I get to draw stuff.

Y ou want to be friends? Okay.

Murray Munro (8)
Jordanhill School, Glasgow

78

Swimming

S wimming is my favourite hobby.
W ater splishes and splashes.
I love to swim and I love to dive.
M anaging to swim takes practice.
M akes me very happy and excited.
I enjoy it so much.
N ever ever will I hate it.
G iving me swimming skills.

Raya McLaughlin (7)
Jordanhill School, Glasgow

Football

F ootball is amazing, I love it.

O h Ronaldo is amazing.

O h Messi is a god!

T hiago Silva is really good.

B ecoming a footballer is a bit hard.

A nd when I grow up I want to be a footballer.

L ovely sport that keeps you fit.

L oud crowds.

Aidan McLaughlin (7)

Jordanhill School, Glasgow

Swimming

S wimming is my favourite hobby.
W hen I swim I float.
I love swimming.
M y swimming lessons are fun.
M e and my family are good at swimming.
I 'm happy with swimming.
N o one drowns.
G ood things happen in the water.

Zara Patel (7)
Jordanhill School, Glasgow

Nintendo

N intendo is the best

I love making Lego

N intendo Switch is the best

T itanic is my second favourite boat ever

E gypt is the best place ever

N ice is ketchup on a hot dog.

D elicious cheesy burgers

O siris was a god.

Arran Bailey (7)
Jordanhill School, Glasgow

Football

F ootball is fun

O n the pitch you score goals.

O ver and over I practise

T he thing I like most is scoring.

B lack football boots

A t football, you pass the ball

L ots of fun

L ooking at fans.

Brody Doran (7)

Jordanhill School, Glasgow

Freya

F luffy and cute puppies are my favourite animals.

R abbits are my second favourite animals as long as they are really fluffy.

E xciting Brownies.

Y iyi is my best friend, we play lots of fun games together.

A mazing Spanish.

Freya Mackay (7)

Jordanhill School, Glasgow

Skate

S kateboarding is my favourite hobby.

K angaroos are my third favourite animal.

A rt is something I do when it's raining.

T omato sauce and olives are my favourite toppings on pizza.

E va is my name and I am kind.

Eva Dougan (8)

Jordanhill School, Glasgow

Swimming

S wimming is my hobby.
W ater makes me think.
I magination on holiday.
M y favourite stroke is front.
M uscles moving.
I n the water.
N ice cool water.
G azing at the sparkling roof.

Sam McDonald (7)
Jordanhill School, Glasgow

School

S eamus is my name
C ats are fluffy and my favourite pet
H ome is my favourite place
O h no, I have to get out of bed
O h no, I have to get changed for school
L et's go to breakfast.

Seamus Farrell (7)
Jordanhill School, Glasgow

Lawrie

L ego is one of my favourite things.

A iden is one of my friends.

W riting is really fun.

R eading books is cool.

I think I am funny.

E ven when it's raining I am still happy.

Lawrie Nairn (7)

Jordanhill School, Glasgow

Things About Me

S wimming is my hobby, it is so much fun.

A little bit of football cheers me up.

R aya is my best friend, she helps me when I am down.

A ll the things make me happy, nothing makes me sad.

Sara Aslam (7)
Jordanhill School, Glasgow

Thomas

T his is me!

H i, my name is Thomas.

O ne six-year-old brother and cat.

M ommy has really long hair.

A lexander is my friend.

S eamus is also my friend.

Thomas Burke (8)
Jordanhill School, Glasgow

Blue

B lue is my dog, he is bluey-black, he's small and fluffy.

L ego is his sneaky snack

U nique is Blue, yes he is

E ven though Blue is cute and fluffy, he can be naughty.

Alexander Matheson (7)

Jordanhill School, Glasgow

My Happy Acrostic Poem

A rt is my favourite thing.
R unning is my favourite sport.
W hen I come home I feel happy.
E very day I feel happy.
N ever be mean.

Arwen Gilmour (7)
Jordanhill School, Glasgow

Erik

E xcellent at dividing and multiplying.

R ed flames burning, flames are super cool.

I cy winters are my favourite.

K ind to everyone.

Erik Tilston (7)
Jordanhill School, Glasgow

Piano

P ractise every night

I ndoor and outdoor

A nd I love it

N oise is everywhere

O f course I won't stop.

Chloe Turnbull (7)
Jordanhill School, Glasgow

Colourful

C olours of the rainbow make me happy.

O h no I like lots of colours.

L ove lots of rainbows.

O h these colours make me excited.

U nicorns make me happy.

R ainbows are so cool.

F unny makes me laugh.

U nicorns are cool.

L ove watermelons.

Dulcine-Vittoria Dubceac (6)

St John's CE School, Stanmore

Football

F eet are used to play football

O ther team are going to win

O verall Liverpool is the best

T all players

B all needs power

A lways be a good team member.

L earning ways how to win matches.

L earning a new position.

Reheem Khan (7)
St John's CE School, Stanmore

Deumini

D eumini is my name.

E nd of my name there is an E.

U nicorn is my favourite animal.

M um helps me with my studies at home.

I n my home I study a lot.

N ight is when I go to sleep.

I n my home I tell my mum to go to the park.

Deumini Kolonne Appuhamillage (5)

St John's CE School, Stanmore

Football

F ootball is so fun.

O n the playground.

O n the playground or anywhere.

T his is so easy

B ut for some it's hard.

A lways rough. If you're

L ittle it's easier to play.

L ike for some it's hard.

Emma Stone (7)
St John's CE School, Stanmore

Lemon

L emons are sour and I like it.

E ven though no one else likes it except for my mum we still eat it.

M um likes it also with water and I do the same.

O n some days I eat lemon or lemon and water.

N o one else likes it except for me and Mum.

Rio Reyes-Francis (6)
St John's CE School, Stanmore

Agastya

A gastya is my name.

G rapes are my favourite fruit.

A lia is my best friend.

S wimming I like.

T rying to be kind and take our time.

Y ellow is my favourite colour.

A sking questions when I don't know the answer.

Agastya Panwar (6)

St John's CE School, Stanmore

St John's

S ophisticated school.
T alented school in their music.

J oyful school staff.
O nly school that's perfect for me.
H appy school-teaching teachers.
N ice and kind school.
'S uper grateful for my school.

Sophia Murphy (6)
St John's CE School, Stanmore

Swimming

S unshine outside.
W ater inside the swimming pool.
I nside water I dive.
M y clothes are wet.
M e in the swimming pool.
I nside the class I learn to swim.
N o splashing allowed.
G o swimming.

Sebastian Onate (6)
St John's CE School, Stanmore

Pokémon

P ikachu has electric powers.

O ak trees are around.

K ey, key, keys all around.

É evee! I like that!

M o, my name is Mo.

O h I forgot that.

N o, no, no I don't want a Pokéball.

David Alexandru (6)
St John's CE School, Stanmore

Chelsea

C ool footballers
H ome, Stamford Bridge
E legant César Azpilicueta
L earning new tricks to score goals
S mart Thomas Tuchel
E lephants are worse than Chelsea
A good Chelsea squad.

Alexander Boghian (7)
St John's CE School, Stanmore

Iustina

I like my teacher.
U nder the bed is my favourite place.
S ummer is my favourite season.
T eigan is my friend.
I love my mum.
N ever give up.
A beautiful butterfly cheers me up.

Iustina Chelaru (6)
St John's CE School, Stanmore

Sisters

S isters are joyful

I love my sisters

S assy but cute

T urns around when I'm talking

E nters the room without knocking

R eally wriggles about

S ays I'm annoying.

Ava-Grace Lucien (7)

St John's CE School, Stanmore

Aaliyah

A lways being kind.

A aliyah is my name.

L earning is my favourite.

I love my pets.

Y ellow is my favourite colour.

A lways help people.

H opping is what I like to do.

Aaliyah Perkins (6)

St John's CE School, Stanmore

Ishaan

I shaan is my name.
S illy jokes make me laugh.
H appy people make me excited.
A pineapple is my favourite fruit.
A hedgehog is my favourite animal.
N azil is my friend.

Ishaan Wara (6)
St John's CE School, Stanmore

Aileen

A lways being kind.
I am very careful with what I am saying.
L ove my family.
E very day I learn.
E verything I do my family appreciate.
N ever be late for school.

Aileen Grigore (7)
St John's CE School, Stanmore

Jigglypuff

J iggly like jelly
I am funky
G iggling a lot
G uggling a lot
L oudly
Y ummy yummy
P uffy
U nicorn theme
F unky
F at.

Eli Nistor (7)
St John's CE School, Stanmore

Bhavik

B havik is my name.

H elping is what I do.

A nimals are good.

V ans are what I like to learn about.

I can help my friends.

K angaroos are my favourite animal.

Bhavik Benoi (5)
St John's CE School, Stanmore

Bunny

B ig, fluffy bunny jumping around
U nder in their hole
N ice little bunny sleeping in their hole
N um num num, carrots are yum
Y ay! This animal is full of energy.

Zaynab Moledina (7)
St John's CE School, Stanmore

Kenya

K ilimanjaro is the tallest mountain in Africa.

E ndangered species are in Kenya.

N airobi is the capital.

Y es, I will go to Kenya.

A griculture is important.

Chisom Eziefula (7)

St John's CE School, Stanmore

Funny

F ull of fun and happiness.
U tterly smiley always.
N ot very tall but very cute.
N ice, kind, clever and beautiful.
Y ou are amazing Anna-Maria.

Anna-Maria Matyas (6)
St John's CE School, Stanmore

Tennis

T errific sport.

E veryone should play tennis.

N ice and fun every time.

N ever give up.

I n a stadium with a crowd.

S erve is great!

Lydia Tapp (7)
St John's CE School, Stanmore

Reign

R ain is the best because you get to splash in puddles.
E very day I go to school.
I love my teachers.
G od is the best.
N ever give up.

Reign Maleek Huie (6)
St John's CE School, Stanmore

Lions

L ions are fast.
I n the jungle they eat a lot of meat.
O n the safari I see the lions.
N o one wants to see lions.
S o they go home.

Nicolas Gavril (6)
St John's CE School, Stanmore

Burger

B est friends forever.
U pstairs sometimes.
R estaurant is busy.
G ood with chips.
E at now and again.
R eally filling.

Alexandru Buburuza (7)
St John's CE School, Stanmore

Noble

N oble is my name.

O range is my favourite colour.

B eing nice to my new class.

L earning new things.

E very day is full of hugs.

Noble Owusu Nyamekye (6)

St John's CE School, Stanmore

James

J ames is my name.

A nimals like me.

M y best friend is Ishan.

E very day I hug Mummy and Dad.

S howing kindness to all.

James Nicoll (6)

St John's CE School, Stanmore

Aadya

A adya is my name.

A mber colour is my favourite.

D addy is the best.

Y ummy apples make me happy.

A nimals are amazing.

Aadya Mishra (6)
St John's CE School, Stanmore

Spider

S uperhero

P romises to Iron Man

I ncredible

D ecorated suit

E lectric gadgets

R ecommended hero.

Damian Pascal (6)
St John's CE School, Stanmore

Kind

K indness is what I like to show.

I like to eat ice cream.

N ewts are my favourite animal.

D ulane is my best friend.

Eva Brindusoiu (6)
St John's CE School, Stanmore

Cats

C ats are cute and fluffy.
A t night-time they like to play.
T he cats eat too much.
S o they sleep every day.

James Sav (6)
St John's CE School, Stanmore

Gaming

G aming eyes

A mong us

M agikarp

I vysaur

N intendo Switch

G olden Magikarp.

Shaheem Ramzan (7)
St John's CE School, Stanmore

The Bright Golden Sun

S hining sun
U p in the sky
N ice and warm
N ot raining today
Y ellow gold, bright sun.

Kulthum Moledina (7)
St John's CE School, Stanmore

Happy

H appy is my friend.
A pple.
P retty dresses.
P olite.
Y es, I am happy.

Ameliya Powell Clarke
St John's CE School, Stanmore

Fish

F ishy and beautiful

I t is happy

S he's in the sea

H iding from sharks.

Rayan McAlister (6)
St John's CE School, Stanmore

Dad

D ashing dad I have got.
A superhero dad I have got.
D ay or night he is the best.

Damaris Vladean (7)
St John's CE School, Stanmore

Dogs

D ogs are so cute.
O ld and cheeky.
G olden brown.
S mart and little.

Keziah O (6)
St John's CE School, Stanmore

Home

H ot food

O n the couch

M akes Mom mad

E very day.

George Raine (6)

St John's CE School, Stanmore

Beautiful

B eautiful butterfly flying in the air.

E xciting kittens play together.

A dorable babies in your eyes.

U rwa plays with you.

T ag your friend.

I like to play with my friend.

F ull of new friends.

U seful, cute kittens.

L ovely world in our town.

Urwa Azmat (7)
Wincham Community Primary School, Wincham

Ice Cream

I ce cream is the best dessert.
C one is crunchy.
E ating ice cream is the best.

C ouch sitting eating ice cream.
R ight at the table is where I eat.
E veryone eats ice cream.
A mazing at eating ice cream.
M aking it is easy.

Rory Harris (7)
Wincham Community Primary School, Wincham

Football

F ootball is the best.

O llie is a good friend.

O ne and only Mbappé

T eammates help you win

B icycle kicks are a good skill

A t half-time, you have a break.

L ongshot is a 1% chance of a goal.

L ots of people like football.

Hugo Moorhouse (7)

Wincham Community Primary School, Wincham

Ronaldo

R onaldo is amazing.

O riginally Ronaldo played for Sporting Lisbon.

N o one is as good as him.

A nyone want to challenge me?

L ots of people watch him play.

D ouglas, my friend, likes Ronaldo.

O tters are Ronaldo's favourite animal.

Sebastian Fitzsimmons (6)
Wincham Community Primary School, Wincham

Ice Cream

I eat ice cream.
C old ice cools me down.
E xciting ice cream.

C reamy ice cream is delicious.
R ed strawberry ice cream is the best.
E very ice cream is the best.
A mazing ice cream.
M essy ice cream.

Lucy Stainsby (7)
Wincham Community Primary School, Wincham

Football

F ootball is the best.
O llie is a show-off.
O llie is a good striker.
T eammates help you to win.
B est footballer.
A lways listen to the coach.
L egs help you to run.
L ots of people play football.

Oliver Earl (7)

Wincham Community Primary School, Wincham

Ice Cream

I am the best.
C allum is my name.
E ating ice cream is the best.

C ute is what I am.
R ed is my favourite colour.
E xcited when it is in my hands.
A mazing ice cream is good.
M essy food.

Callum Scott (6)
Wincham Community Primary School, Wincham

Squirrels

S quirrels are intelligent.

Q uarrel sometimes.

U nusual creatures.

I looked up at the sky and I saw a squirrel.

R elaxing squirrels are peaceful.

R ed squirrels are cool.

E at nuts.

L ike nuts.

Joshua Southern (6)

Wincham Community Primary School, Wincham

Disney

D isney is amazing.

I t has lots of characters.

S parkling fireworks in the sky.

N ice parades start in the evening.

E xciting smiles come on people's faces.

Y ummy dinner and breakfast is served for you any time.

Scarlett Clayton (6)

Wincham Community Primary School, Wincham

Swimming

S wimming is fun.

W ish I was seven.

I am a friend to Teddy.

M y dad helps me.

M cDonald's to take home.

I ndiana is my name.

N ice underwater.

G ames in the swimming pool.

Indiana Bunby (6)

Wincham Community Primary School, Wincham

Sharing

S ienna is my friend.

H arper is my name.

A friend of mine is kind.

R ed pandas are my favourite animal.

I am kind and nice.

N ice and kind.

G eorge is my friend.

Harper Morgan (6)

Wincham Community Primary School, Wincham

Me

J oining in with my playing.
O rla and Floppy are my best friends.
S haring my smile with everyone.
H appy and helping every day.
U pset without my friends.
A lways keep busy.

Joshua Macnair (5)
Wincham Community Primary School, Wincham

Ocelots

O celots are speedy,
C lever and scary.
E veryone is scared of them.
L ove meat.
O ne very dangerous animal.
T hey are full of fabulous spots.
S parkling eyes.

Lucy Carson (7)
Wincham Community Primary School, Wincham

Animals

A nimals are adorable.

N aughty sometimes.

I like animals.

M y favourite animals are cats.

A nimals are magic.

L ovely.

S ome animals are cheeky.

Annabelle Sutton (7)

Wincham Community Primary School, Wincham

Puppies

P uppies are my favourite.
U nicorns are cute.
P roud of my writing.
P erfect reading.
I like Chinese food.
E vie is my name.
S nakes are scary.

Evie North (6)

Wincham Community Primary School, Wincham

Maddie

M y favourite colour is pink.
A lways smiling and happy.
D ogs are my favourite animal.
D ogs are the best.
I love my dad.
E veryone loves me.

Maddie Silva (6)

Wincham Community Primary School, Wincham

Corgi

C orgis are the Queen's dogs.
O bviously they are very fluffy.
R eally cute and good company.
G ood pets.
I love corgis because they are my friends.

Eudora Hill-Alexander (7)
Wincham Community Primary School, Wincham

Marcus

M arcus plays for Harlequins
A cat and dog is like Marcus
R eally like rugby
C an Marcus kick?
U p is where Marcus kicks
S porty Marcus.

George Travis (6)

Wincham Community Primary School, Wincham

Cheetah

C ats are nice.

H e is my brother.

E xciting dogs.

E verybody is nice to me.

T he best animal.

A ged five.

H as a big family.

Freya McGarr (5)

Wincham Community Primary School, Wincham

Fish

F ish are my pets.

I f I feel lonely I go to my fish and they make me feel better.

S o fish are very fast swimmers.

H ave you got adorable, cute guppies?

Oliver Harrison (6)

Wincham Community Primary School, Wincham

Sienna

S ienna is my name.

I like McDonald's.

E veryone is my friend.

N ice and kind.

N obody is the same.

A pril Fool's Day.

Sienna Lane (6)
Wincham Community Primary School, Wincham

Funny

F avourite dog is a husky.

U nicorns are my favourite.

N annie is the best.

N annie gives me McDonald's.

"Y es!" said Emily.

Alice Kerr (6)
Wincham Community Primary School, Wincham

Babies

B abies are my favourite.
A Nintendo is cool.
B irthday is in April.
I like kittens.
E vie is my friend.
S illy friend.

Jake Jennings (6)
Wincham Community Primary School, Wincham

Callum

C allum is my brother.

A boy is my friend.

L ove my brother.

L ook cute.

U ses a book.

M akes eggs with Mum.

Jake Noden (6)
Wincham Community Primary School, Wincham

Kacie

K indness is my superpower.
A mazing me.
C an be an amazing friend.
I love my dog, Archie.
E veryone can be my friend.

Kacie Pregnall (7)
Wincham Community Primary School, Wincham

Earth

E arth is where we live.

A mazing Earth is ours.

R elaxing Earth.

T itan is nice.

H appy Earth forever!

Alexander Newman (7)

Wincham Community Primary School, Wincham

Loky

L oky is lovely.

O bviously the best dog in the world.

K indness is Loky's superpower.

Y ou will love Loky.

Douglas McGarr (7)
Wincham Community Primary School, Wincham

Tayla

T ayla is my sister.
A rla is my name.
Y ou are my friend.
L ovely friend.
A mazing at smiling.

Arla Gibson-Clarke (6)
Wincham Community Primary School, Wincham

Daisy

D aisy and dogs.
A rla is a friend.
I like reading.
S porty me.
Y ou are smiley.

Daisy Butterworth (6)
Wincham Community Primary School, Wincham

Pugs

P ugs are perfect.

U seful for cleaning up food.

G entle and cute.

S illy pugs.

Penelope Challinor (7)
Wincham Community Primary School, Wincham

Art

A rt can be done on a canvas.

R eally colourful palette.

T idy up when you're done.

Evie Wright (7)

Wincham Community Primary School, Wincham

Nice

N ice to Daisy.

I am kind.

C an play with my dad.

E veryone is kind to me.

Teddy Cooke (5)
Wincham Community Primary School, Wincham

Young Writers Information

We hope you have enjoyed reading this book – and that you will continue to in the coming years.

If you're the parent or family member of an enthusiastic poet or story writer, do visit
www.youngwriters.co.uk/subscribe
and sign up to receive news, competitions, writing challenges and tips, activities and much, much more! There's lots to keep budding writers motivated!

If you would like to order further copies of this book, or any of our other titles, then please give us a call or order via your online account.

Young Writers
Remus House
Coltsfoot Drive
Peterborough
PE2 9BF
(01733) 890066
info@youngwriters.co.uk

Join in the conversation!
Tips, news, giveaways and much more!

f YoungWritersUK **🐦** YoungWritersCW **📷** youngwriterscw